Wildfires

By Pam McDowell

AV² provides enriched content that supplements and complements this book. Weigl's AV² books strive to create inspired learning and engage young minds in a total learning experience.

Your AV² Media Enhanced books come alive with...

 Audio
Listen to sections of the book read aloud.

 Key Words
Study vocabulary, and complete a matching word activity.

 Video
Watch informative video clips.

 Quizzes
Test your knowledge.

 Embedded Weblinks
Gain additional information for research.

 Slide Show
View images and captions, and prepare a presentation.

 Try This!
Complete activities and hands-on experiments.

... and much, much more!

Go to **www.av2books.com**, and enter this book's unique code.

BOOK CODE

C 7 1 7 2 3 8

AV² by Weigl brings you media enhanced books that support active learning.

Published by AV² by Weigl
350 5th Avenue, 59th Floor
New York, NY 10118
Websites: www.av2books.com   www.weigl.com

Library of Congress Control Number: 2014934888
ISBN 978-1-4896-1222-9 (hardcover)
ISBN 978-1-4896-1223-6 (softcover)
ISBN 978-1-4896-1224-3 (single-user eBook)
ISBN 978-1-4896-1225-0 (multi-user eBook)

Printed in the United States of America in North Mankato, Minnesota
1 2 3 4 5 6 7 8 9 0 18 17 16 15 14

062014
WEP090514

Senior Editor: Aaron Carr
Art Director: Terry Paulhus

Contents

Wildfires Are one of the Deadliest Disasters in the World

Fire is part of the natural environment. Fire burns dead branches and fallen trees, which releases **nutrients** into the soil. With the right conditions, though, fire can burn out of control. A wildfire is a large, fierce fire capable of burning millions of acres (hectares) of forest, grassland, or agricultural land. A wildfire can move quickly, burning homes and even entire towns.

Wildfires burn on every continent except Antarctica. Areas that are hot and sunny with low **humidity** and strong winds often have wildfires. The desert-like conditions in Australia, southern Africa, and parts of California are perfect for wildfires. Even places that are thought to be cold, such as Alaska, can be threatened by wildfires during the summer.

Wildfires are a natural disaster, but they are different from earthquakes, floods, or tornadoes. People cannot stop these other disasters, but wildfires can be fought. Technology is improving to help people put out these fires more quickly and safely. Even more importantly, unlike other natural disasters, people are often the cause of wildfires.

First responders often name wildfires after things they see nearby, such as a creek, river, or city. There are no rules for naming a wildfire.

A conflagration, or large wildfire, is able to change the weather in the surrounding areas.

Most wildfires Are Caused by People

A fire needs three things in order to burn. These are fuel, high temperature, and oxygen. Together, these make up what is known as the "fire triangle." The fuel that a wildfire needs is dry **deadfall**, brush, or grass. High temperatures can be caused by a heat wave, and air provides the oxygen. The world's worst wildfires have taken place after long **droughts**, when there is little moisture in the air, soil, or plants. The worst wildfires have happened during heat waves that have raised temperatures to record highs. Winds push the flames along with fresh oxygen. These conditions make it easy for a small fire, or even a spark, to grow into a wildfire.

TYPES OF WILDFIRES

Surface Fires	Crown Fires	Ground Fires	Prescribed Fire
This type of wildfire burns deadfall on the forest floor or grass and brush in more open areas. As the fire grows, it moves to taller vegetation and the tops of trees, or tree crowns.	This type of wildfire is often started by lightning. It burns the tops of trees and is easily blown by the wind. Crown fires spread faster than any other type of wildfire.	This type of wildfire burns **organic** material, such as peat, below the surface of the forest floor or grassland. A ground fire is the slowest moving but most destructive kind of wildfire. It is difficult to control and often burns for a long period of time.	This type of fire may be set for several reasons. A small, controlled fire will reduce the deadfall in a natural area and provide nutrients for other plants. Farmers burn areas of cropland to prepare it for planting. However, if these fires get out of control, they may become wildfires.

Lightning strikes often cause forest fires. Some of these may become wildfires if the conditions are right. Most often, though, **ignition** is caused by people. Sparks from machinery, hot motors, and campfires can start fires. A controlled burn in hot and dry conditions may spread out of control and become a wildfire. Sometimes, fires are caused by **arson**. These fires are set with the goal of causing damage or harm.

On average, about 1.2 million acres (485,000 hectares) of woodland burns each year in the United States.

Natural Causes
lightning, volcanic eruptions

Lightning strikes the Earth 100,000 times a day.

FIRE STARTERS
10-20% of these lightning strikes cause fire.

In 2012, 9,443 wildfires were caused by lightning in the United States.

VS

Human Causes
carelessness, sparks from machinery, cigarettes, arson

In 2012, **58,381** wildfires were caused by people in the United States

Indonesian wildfires started by farmers in **1997** cost more than **$6 billion** to put out.

Wildfires Can Be Fought and Prevented

In 1910, a wildfire burned more than 3 million acres (1.2 million ha) in Idaho, Montana, and Washington. This fire is known as the "Big Burn." The fire started as several smaller fires, which were ignited by lightning and the careless actions of people. Members of the U.S. Forest Service, the military, and 4,000 firefighters fought the blaze for three days. They took shelter in creek beds and mine shafts when the fire raged out of control. Rain finally extinguished the wildfire.

The Big Burn changed the way Americans thought about forest fire. The National Forest Service had been started in 1905 to manage the country's forests. After the fire, the National Forest Service was determined to prevent and extinguish all fires, even small, natural fires. This practice continued for decades. Later, research began to show the benefits of fire in nature. The first laboratory for wildfire research opened in Georgia in 1959. Later, others opened in Montana (1960), California (1963), and Washington (2003). Scientists study how fire spreads and how to protect people, homes, and businesses.

In some cases, dead leaves or trees can create enough to suddenly burst into flames. This is called spontaneous combustion. These fires are most likely to happen in extremely hot and dry weather.

FIRE DANGER EXTREME TODAY!

The facemask that firefighters wear is called a Self Contained Breathing Apparatus (SCBA). The attached air tank provides the firefighter with between 30 to 45 minutes of air.

In dry conditions, finding a fire early can help prevent it from growing into a wildfire. Trained professionals and volunteers use tower lookouts, aircraft, and satellites to watch for fires. Technology such as remote control television, high resolution photography, heat-sensing devices, and radar have improved the success of early wildfire detection.

Once a wildfire is spotted, firefighters work to keep it from growing. First, they slow and stop the spread of fire. Then, they put out the fire. The goal is to make sure the fire causes as little damage as possible. To do this, firefighters must break the fire triangle either by removing the fuel or by reducing the temperature or oxygen feeding the fire. Water is often used to extinguish fires, but it is not always available at the scene of a wildfire. Firefighters may use dirt to extinguish a fire instead. Chemicals such as **retardants** are dropped onto the fire from aircraft.

Fighting wildfires is a dangerous job. Incident Meteorologists (IMETs) are weather experts in the National Weather Service. They work with firefighters as they battle wildfires. IMETs track wildfires and report information about the fires and weather conditions. Their goal is to make sure the firefighters are safe.

Wildfires Are a Global Issue

S atellite images show that there is always a fire burning somewhere in the world. Africa suffers the largest and most frequent burns. More than half of all wildfires happen in Africa, most often in the countries between the **Tropic of Cancer** and the **Tropic of Capricorn**. In this area, grasslands and agricultural fields burn easily. People there have used fire to prepare the land for planting crops for centuries. However, long droughts and heat waves make this practice dangerous.

Farmers in many other parts of the world use similar methods to prepare their fields. In Asia, the largest fire in Indonesia's history was started by accident in 1997. Farmers had set a series of small fires to clear land for palm oil and rubber plantations. The fires grew out of control and burned 12 million acres (5 million ha) of land. Only 50 percent of that was agricultural land. The other 50 percent was forest and grassland that was not intended to be burned.

In some African countries, slash and burn farming is practiced. This involves cutting down and burning forest land to create new farmland.

In 2007, the area of Alaska's North Slope experienced its hottest weather in 129 years. During this time, there was 20 percent less rainfall than normal. When lightning ignited the Anaktuvuk River wildfire, it burned for almost three months. More than 247,000 acres (100,000 ha) of **tundra** were burned. A similar heat wave in Russia in 2010 pushed temperatures up to 100 °Fahrenheit (38 °Celsius). It was the hottest and driest summer since 1890. There were many fires, which destroyed 34 million acres (14 million ha) in total. This included one quarter of Russia's grain crop.

Seasonal winds such as El Niño can cause extreme wildfires in coastal areas. In California, the Santa Ana winds are often blamed for fires that threaten cities and destroy huge areas of grassland and forest. These hot, dry winds blow during the fall and early winter, usually after a hot summer that has left vegetation dry and highly flammable. The Santa Ana winds push clouds of embers far ahead of the fire. This causes the fire to spread across **firebreaks**, burning as much as 1,000 acres (404 ha) per hour.

Firefighters create firebreaks by clearing vegetation. Firebreaks are used to starve the fire by removing its source of fuel.

3:03 PM

is the average time that fires are reported in Yellowstone National Park because fires burn more strongly in hot, mid-day sunlight.

LAND BURN

185 million to more than 2 billion acres (75–820 million ha) of land burn each year worldwide.

Together, **64 countries** reported 487,000 vegetation fires each year from 2003 to 2007.

More than 55,000 people died from smog or heat during Russia's fires of 2010.

All-Time Records

G athering information about past wildfires and environmental conditions helps scientists predict where future wildfires may take place.

DEADLIEST

More than 1,200 people died in the Peshtigo Fire that burned 3.7 million acres (1.5 million ha) in Wisconsin and Michigan in 1871. The fire was sparked by railroad workers clearing land.

MOST FIREFIGHTERS

More than 10,000 firefighters, 2,000 soldiers, and 3,000 additional people worked to extinguish the Russian wildfires of 2010.

BIGGEST BURN

Nearly 5 million acres (2.2 million ha) burned during Australia's Black Friday Bushfires in 1939. "Bushfire" is what Australians call wildfires.

LARGEST EVACUATION

Nearly one million people were **evacuated** during the California wildfires of 2007. At least 1,500 homes were destroyed.

Wildfires in the United States

O n average, there are more than 100,000 wildfires in the United States each year. Most of the 50 states experience wildfires. The western states report the most wildfires, especially California. In these states, the wildfire season is 78 days longer than it was 15 years ago. More people live in or close to natural areas where wildfires take place. As a result, 10 times more structures have been burned in wildfires since 2000 than in the 1960s. Many wildfires today cause billions of dollars in damages.

WILDLAND FIRE POTENTIAL

| VERY LOW |
| LOW |
| MODERATE |
| HIGH |
| VERY HIGH |

Pacific Ocean

MAP SCALE

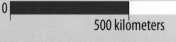

0   500 miles
500 kilometers

North Dakota

Minnesota

South Dakota

Nebraska

Kansas

Oklahoma

Texas

Iowa

Missouri

Arkansas

Louisiana

Wisconsin

Illinois

Indiana

Kentucky

Tennessee

Mississippi

Alabama

Lake
Superior

Lake
Michigan

Lake
Huron

Michigan

Ohio

West
Virginia

Georgia

Florida

Lake Erie

Lake
Ontario

New York

Pennsylvania

Virginia

North Carolina

South Carolina

New Hampshire

Vermont

Maine

Massachusetts

Rhode Island

Connecticut

New Jersey

Delaware

Maryland

Atlantic
Ocean

Gulf of
Mexico

Australia Experiences the most Wildfires of any Country in the World

More than 70 percent of Australia is desert or semi-desert. In 2009, a long drought and summer heat wave created the perfect conditions for a wildfire. The Black Saturday Bushfires began on Saturday, February 7. They burned until March 14. In total, 1.1 million acres (440,00 ha) and 3,500 structures were burned, and 173 people died.

Like California, bushfires in Australia often threaten areas where people live and work. Three large bushfires threatened to combine into one conflagration in October 2013. The largest fire had a front 190 miles (300 kilometers) wide. It was only a two-hour drive from Sydney, the country's largest city and home to more than 4.6 million people. More than 1,200 firefighters and 83 aircraft worked to extinguish the fire before it reached the city.

A wildfire can move at speeds of 14 miles (22 km) an hour.

It takes a great deal of highly trained people and expensive equipment to fight wildfires. Countries have begun to work together to help fight these fires. In 2000, more than 500 people from Australia, Canada, New Zealand, and Mexico helped fight wildfires in the United States. The National Interagency Fire Center coordinates these projects in the U.S. Wildfire specialists travel around the world, moving from one emergency to the next. In 2008, 44 Australian operation specialists helped coordinate the fight against the fires in northern California. Just a few months later, in February 2009, the United States sent 73 fire personnel to Australia during the Black Saturday Bushfires. Later that same year, a U.S. management team and 20 smokejumpers traveled to Canada to fight wildfires in British Columbia.

The smokejumper program began in 1939 but the first fire jump was not made until 1940.

75% of the state of Victoria
was affected by the fires and smoke of the **Black Friday Bushfires** in 1939

FASTER than a FOREST FIRE

A forest fire may move up to 10 miles (16 km) per hour, while grass fires can reach 37 miles (60 km) per hour in strong winds.

5 people were arrested on suspicion of starting the fires near Sydney in 2013

Deaths in Australia due to natural disasters 1900 – 201,318 – fire 496, storm 223, landslide 28, flood 314, heat wave 370, earthquake 12, drought 600

The National Fire Rating Danger System

T he National Fire Danger Rating System (NFDRS) was developed in the early 1970s. The goal was to create one system of fire measurement for the entire United States. Using this system helps states communicate with each other when fires cross borders. It also helps when additional support for firefighters is needed.

The Smokey the Bear Wildfire Prevention campaign started in 1944. It is the longest running public service advertising campaign in U.S. history.

The NFDRS is based on the fire triangle. It uses information from thousands of collecting stations across the country. Information on past, current, and predicted weather is used. The NFDRS also tracks how much moisture is in materials that often act as fuel for wildfires. From this information, scientists can estimate when fires in natural areas may take place and how damaging they may be.

National Fire Danger Rating System			
CLASS	**LEVEL**	**COLOR**	**DESCRIPTION**
1	low fire danger	green	Fuels do not ignite easily.
2	moderate fire danger	blue	Fires can start from accidental causes. Grass fires will burn quickly. Wood fires will burn more slowly.
3	high fire danger	yellow	Smaller dead fuels ignite easily. Unattended fires, like campfires, could escape easily. Fire spreads rapidly and is hard to control.
4	very high fire danger	orange	Fires start easily and spread rapidly. **Firebrands** will cause spot fires. Whirlwinds spread sparks and embers. Fire can rarely be fought at the front.
5	extreme	red	Fire is extremely hot and fast, changing directions quickly. This fire can only be fought safely from the sides in order to contain the fire until the weather changes.

Little Known Facts

HIDDEN DANGERS

Evergreens and eucalyptus trees contain oils that can explode into flames in extreme heat.

DANGEROUS JOBS

Hotshots are a team of firefighters whose job is to build a firebreak around a wildfire to keep it from spreading. This often forces them to work directly in the fire's path. Smokejumpers are paratroopers who jump out of planes to get to small fires in hard to reach places. Smokejumpers are used when the threat of a fire spreading is high.

FIRE TORNADO

A large fire can create its own wind. Hot air above the flames rises and cooler air rushes in. This brings more oxygen into the fire. As these winds begin to whirl, a tornado forms, sending embers far ahead of the fire front.

SATELLITE SURVEILLANCE

NASA has two satellites that orbit Earth to record fire activity. One satellite passes over the equator south to north in the afternoon. The other satellite moves over the equator in the opposite direction in the morning. Together, these satellites provide a complete picture of Earth's surface every one to two days.

TOPOGRAPHY MATTERS

Fire spreads quickly uphill and slowly downhill. On a hillside, heat from the fire warms fuel uphill, causing it to burn more quickly when the flames move forward. Winds can push the fire uphill even faster. Winds can also push the fire back downhill. This gives firefighters a better chance to extinguish the flames.

A Wildfire Is Most Dangerous at the Fire Front

Most wildfires are shaped like a teardrop, especially if wind is driving the fire forward. The fire front burns the fastest and hottest. This is the most dangerous place for firefighters. The sides of the fire are called the fire flanks. If the wind changes direction, the upwind flank of the fire will burn extremely fast and may become the fire front. The back of the fire burns the slowest and coolest, with the shortest flames. Generally, the height of a fire's flame is three to five times the height of its fuel.

A firefighter's coat is called a turnout coat. Turnout coats are made of many layers of fire-resistant materials. They can weigh as much as 20 pounds (9 kilograms).

Firefighters can often tell what type of fire is burning from the color of the smoke. Dense, white smoke is created by burning fuel that is very moist. This kind of fire will likely be small and not travel far. Pale grey or blue smoke comes from moist fuel in a fire that travels slowly. Black or dark brown smoke is given off by dry fuel. The fire will burn hotter and travel quickly. Copper or bronze smoke indicates very dry fuel is burning and the fire is likely to spread quickly and cause a great deal of damage.

As the smoke rises, it forms a column that can also provide information about the fire from far away. If the column is thin and rising slowly, the fire is likely small and spreading at low speed. If the column is bent over closer to the ground and increasing in volume, the fire is probably being driven by wind and is spreading quickly.

Smoke from a wildfire is made up of toxic gases, and debris from burning plants and trees.

Wildfires leave the land vulnerable to other disasters

Wildfires can cause problems in an area months or years later. When all vegetation is burned in a fire, the area may flood during heavy rains. Landslides are also likely because there are no trees and other plants left to hold the soil in place. In July 1994, a wildfire burned about 2,000 acres (809 ha) of forest on the slopes of Storm King Mountain in Colorado. Two months later, heavy rains caused a landslide. Tons (metric tons) of mud, rock, and debris poured onto a nearby highway. This buried a 3-mile (5-km) section of the highway.

The Melanophils beetle uses special sensors to search for burning forests. They lay their eggs in the scorched trees after the fire. The dead trees no longer have the natural defenses to prevent the beetle form burrowing.

The smoke from a wildfire can affect people and countries far away from the fire. Ash from the Black Friday Bushfires in Australia in 1939 reached New Zealand, 200 miles (320 km) away. The wildfire in Indonesian in 1994 created smog that spread to the countries of Brunei, Thailand, Vietnam, and the Philippines. Smog can harm people's health. Smog created by wildfires near Moscow in 2010 led to more than 55,000 deaths.

OTHER TYPES OF DISASTERS

Landslide

A landslide happens when rock, earth, and debris move downhill. After a fire burns all vegetation from a hillside, there is little to hold the earth in place. Rain makes the earth heavy. It is pulled downhill by gravity.

Smog

Smog is a combination of smoke and fog that can be dangerous to breathe. The smoke made by wildfires has high levels of dangerous chemicals. These chemicals can irritate a person's throat, eyes, and lungs.

Flooding

Flooding takes place when a an area receives more water than the amount of water the land can absorb. A fire may burn organic matter in the soil, making it less able to hold water. If water cannot filter down into the soil, it collects on the surface and causes a flood.

Gods of Fire in Many Cultures

In ancient times, people believed the universe was made of four basic elements. These were water, air, earth, and fire. People in all parts of the world have myths and legends about fire. Many of these stories are about how people stole fire or were given it as a gift from an animal or god. In Hindu mythology, the god of fire is named Agni. He consumes some things so that other things can live. Agni has great powers and can make his worshippers **immortal**. In one Hindu myth, Agni consumed so many offerings from his worshippers that he became tired. To regain his strength, he burned an entire forest.

In Chinese mythology, Hui Lu is a magician and fire god. He kept 100 firebirds in a gourd. When he set his firebirds loose, he could start a fire across the whole country. In one Chinese myth, Hui Lu is defeated by a princess who appeared in the sky to extinguish his flames with her cloak of mist and dew.

THE STORY OF PROMETHEUS

In Greek mythology, Prometheus was a Titan, or giant. He created humans. Prometheus felt sorry for humans when Zeus forced them to stay on Earth. Prometheus gave fire to humans so they did not have to suffer in cold and darkness or eat raw meat. When he and the humans played a trick on Zeus, the god grew angry and took fire away. Prometheus climbed Olympus and stole a spark that he carried back to the humans. Zeus then punished Prometheus by chaining him to a mountain peak for thousands of years.

Wildfire Timeline

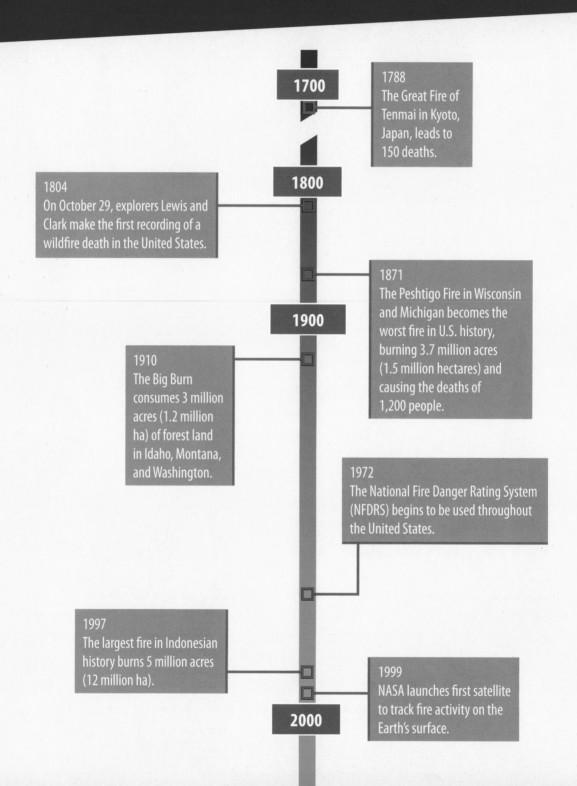

1700

1788
The Great Fire of Tenmai in Kyoto, Japan, leads to 150 deaths.

1800

1804
On October 29, explorers Lewis and Clark make the first recording of a wildfire death in the United States.

1871
The Peshtigo Fire in Wisconsin and Michigan becomes the worst fire in U.S. history, burning 3.7 million acres (1.5 million hectares) and causing the deaths of 1,200 people.

1900

1910
The Big Burn consumes 3 million acres (1.2 million ha) of forest land in Idaho, Montana, and Washington.

1972
The National Fire Danger Rating System (NFDRS) begins to be used throughout the United States.

1997
The largest fire in Indonesian history burns 5 million acres (12 million ha).

1999
NASA launches first satellite to track fire activity on the Earth's surface.

2000

Test Your Knowledge

1 What is the only continent where wildfires do not burn?

A. Antarctica

2 Name the three parts of the 'fire triangle.'

A. Fuel, high temperature, oxygen

3 What are some things firefighters use to extinguish a wildfire?

A. Water, dirt, and retardants

4 What percentage of the world's fires take place in Africa each year?

A. 50 percent

5 On average, how many wildfires take place in the United States each year?

A. 100,000

6 Why does Australia experience the most wildfires of any country in the world?

A. It is 70% desert or semi-desert and often has droughts and high temperatures

7 What does a yellow rating mean in the National Fire Danger Rating System?

A. Fire danger is high, fires start easily, spread rapidly, and are hard to control

8 What are smokejumpers?

A. They are paratroopers who jump out of planes to fight fires in hard to reach places.

9 Will a fire spread more quickly uphill or downhill?

A. Uphill

10 Why is the fire front the most dangerous place for firefighters?

A. It burns the fastest and the hottest

Activity

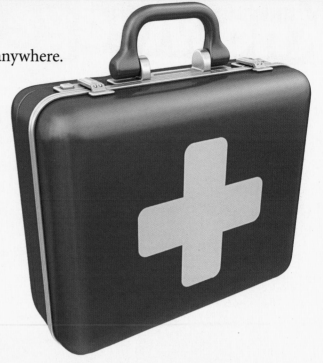

D isasters happen anytime and anywhere. Sadly, when an emergency happens, you may not have much time to respond. The Red Cross says that one way to prepare is by assembling an emergency kit. Once disaster hits, you will not have time to shop or search for supplies.

If you have gathered supplies in advance, your family will be prepared.

1 Know if your home is in a danger zone.

2 Make an evacuation plan. Where will you go? What route will you take to get there? What is an alternate route in case the first route is blocked?

3 Know how to turn off gas, electricity, and water in your home.

4 Know which radio station to listen to for official information about disasters.

5 Build a disaster supply kit.

6 Create an emergency communication plan for getting back together with loved ones if you become separated during a wildfire.

What You Need
• flashlight
• portable, battery-operated radio
• extra batteries
• first aid kit
• emergency food and water
• essential medicines

Key Words

arson: a criminal act of purposely setting property on fire

deadfall: dead branches and tree trunks that lie on the forest floor

droughts: long periods of time without rain

evacuated: moved away from an area to avoid danger

firebrands: pieces of burning wood that may travel a long distance, starting another fire

firebreaks: an object used to stop or slow the spread of a fire

humidity: the amount of moisture in the air

ignition: the act of setting fire to something

immortal: living forever

nutrients: substances needed for growth and good health

organic: something that is made up of living matter

retardants: chemical substances that slow or extinguish fire

Tropic of Cancer: an imaginary line circling the Earth 23 degrees north of the equator

Tropic of Capricorn: an imaginary line circling the Earth 23 degrees south of the equator

tundra: very cold areas in the far north where the ground is always frozen

Index

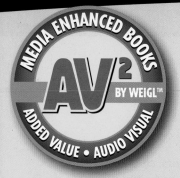
Log on to www.av2books.com

AV² by Weigl brings you media enhanced books that support active learning. Go to www.av2books.com, and enter the special code found on page 2 of this book. You will gain access to enriched and enhanced content that supplements and complements this book. Content includes video, audio, weblinks, quizzes, a slide show, and activities.

AV² Online Navigation

Audio
Listen to sections of the book read aloud.

Book Pages
AV² pages directly correspond to pages in the book.

Video
Watch informative video clips.

Key Words
Study vocabulary, and complete a matching word activity.

Embedded Weblinks
Gain additional information for research.

Quizzes
Test your knowledge.

Slide Show
View images and captions, and prepare a presentation.

Try This!
Complete activities and hands-on experiments.

AMBASSADOR

AV² was built to bridge the gap between print and digital. We encourage you to tell us what you like and what you want to see in the future.

Sign up to be an AV² Ambassador at www.av2books.com/ambassador.